This book belongs to:

_____

_____

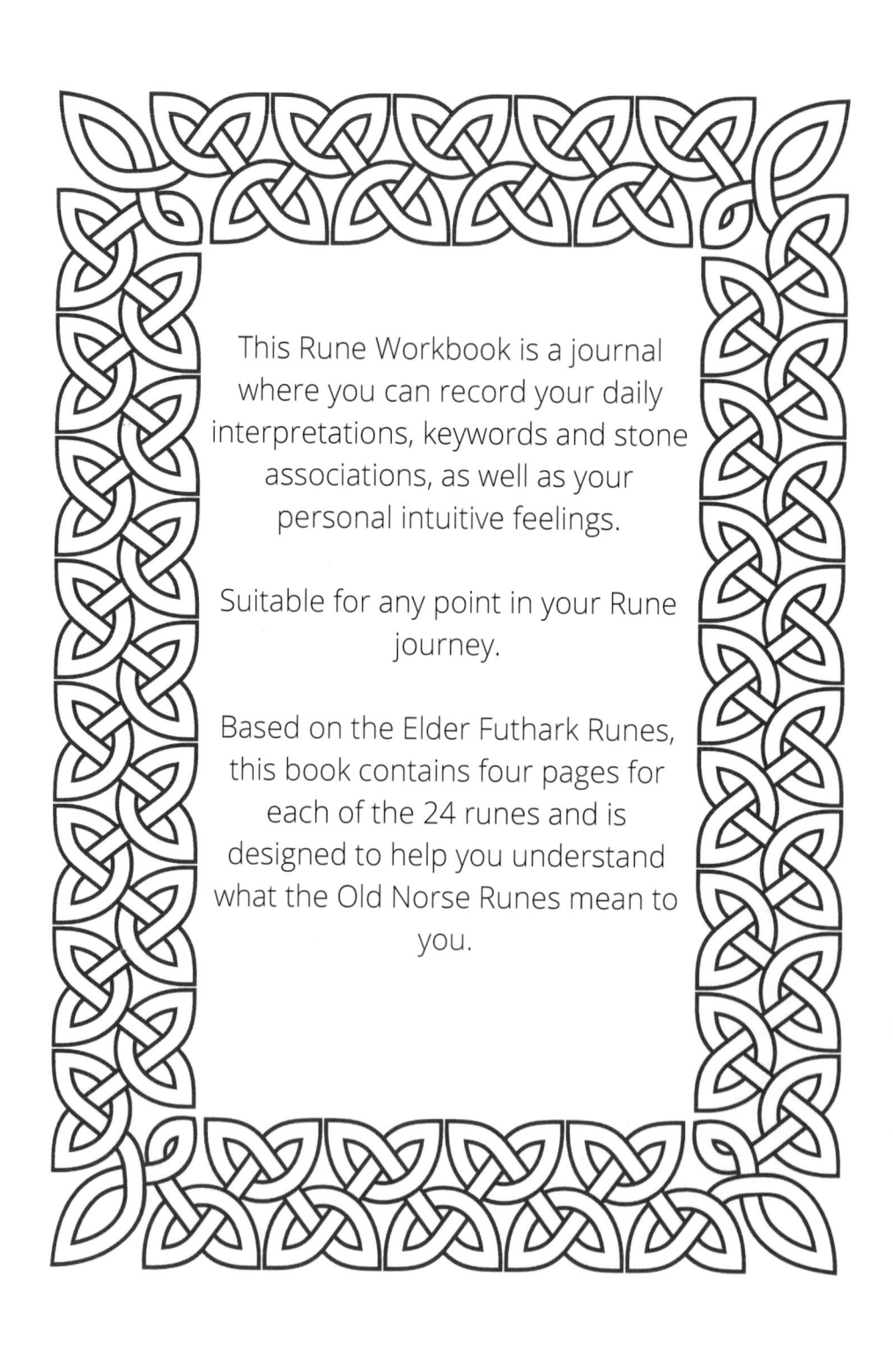

This Rune Workbook is a journal where you can record your daily interpretations, keywords and stone associations, as well as your personal intuitive feelings.

Suitable for any point in your Rune journey.

Based on the Elder Futhark Runes, this book contains four pages for each of the 24 runes and is designed to help you understand what the Old Norse Runes mean to you.

How to use:
In the morning, pull your daily rune, as usual. Then in the evening, reflect on your day using the keywords in the workbook. This will help you intuit what each rune means to you personally.

The workbook is designed to help build your personal interpretations of the stones from a mix of traditional meanings and unique associations that you develop as the runes come up for you again and again during your daily stone pull.

- Use the prompts on each page to guide your evening reflection on the meanings of the runes.
- Record stone keywords
- Add your own intuitive personal meanings
- Use the keywords to describe your day. What did that specific rune mean for you today?

As time passes, you will soon reveal what each stone means for you. This will help you in your personal and public readings.

Rune Workbook

THURISAZ
Thorn

Keywords:
Reaction, Defense, Conflict, Catharsis, Regeneration.

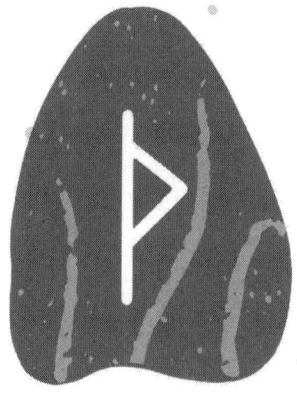

To use this book we recommend pulling a daily stone and journalling in the evening, after reflection of the keywords. How did the rune manifest in your day? See examples below:

01.02.21 — Thurisaz
Alot of conflict and drama today — work was particularly difficult. Collegues were defensive and not hepful.

03.05.21
Had a melt down over the shoe cupboard it frightened the family but I felt better

Copyright © 2021 by Hattie Thorn

All rights reserved. No part of this book may be reproduced or used in any manner without written permission of the copyright owner except for the use of quotations in a book review. For more information, email: hattiethornauthor@gmail.com

FIRST EDITION

Rune Workbook

FEHU
Cattle

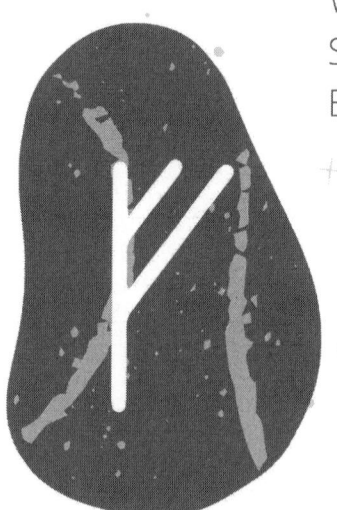

Keywords:

Wealth, Abundance, Success, Security, Fertility, New Beginnings.

Rune Workbook

FEHU
Cattle

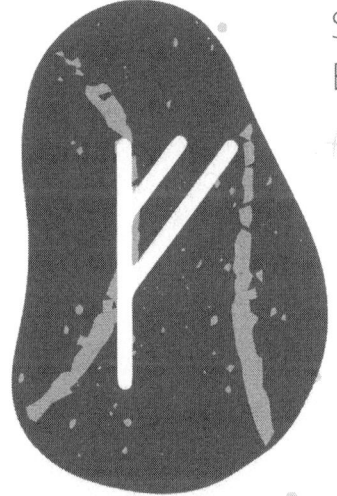

Keywords:

Wealth, Abundance, Success, Security, Fertility, New Beginnings.

_____

_____

_____

_____

_____

_____

_____

_____

Rune Workbook

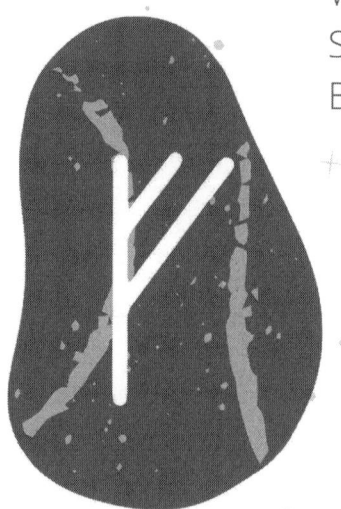

FEHU
Cattle

Keywords:

Wealth, Abundance, Success, Security, Fertility, New Beginnings.

Rune Workbook

FEHU
Cattle

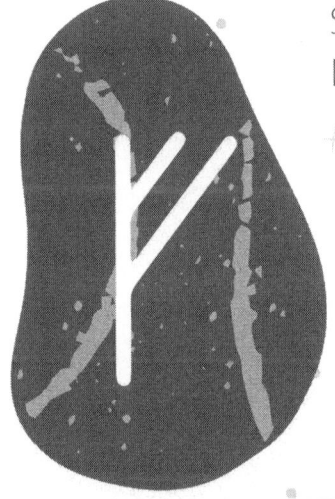

Keywords:

Wealth, Abundance, Success, Security, Fertility, New Beginnings.

_____

_____

_____

_____

_____

_____

_____

_____

RUNE WORKBOOK

URUZ

Ox

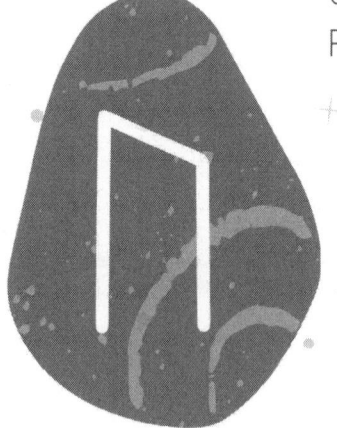

Keywords:

Strength, Tenacity, Courage, Untamed Potential, Freedom, Power.

_____

_____

_____

_____

_____

_____

_____

_____

_____

Rune Workbook

URUZ

Ox

Keywords:

Strength, Tenacity, Courage, Untamed Potential, Freedom, Power.

Rune Workbook

URUZ

Ox

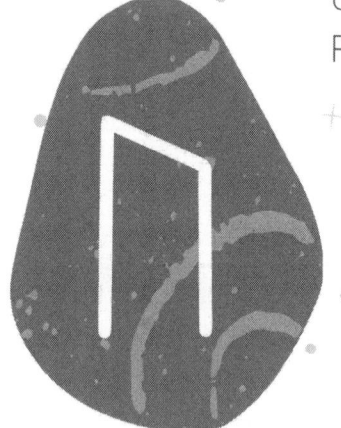

Keywords:

Strength, Tenacity, Courage, Untamed Potential, Freedom, Power.

_____

_____

_____

_____

_____

_____

_____

_____

_____

_____

RUNE WORKBOOK

URUZ

Ox

Keywords:

Strength, Tenacity, Courage, Untamed Potential, Freedom, Power.

Rune Workbook

THURISAZ

Thorn

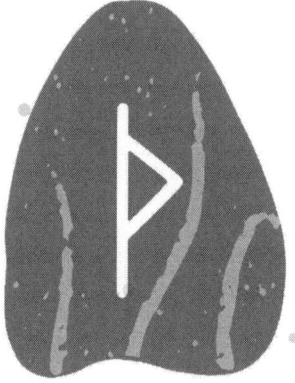

Keywords:

Reaction, Defense, Conflict, Catharsis, Regeneration.

_____

_____

_____

_____

_____

_____

_____

_____

_____

_____

Rune Workbook

THURISAZ

Thorn

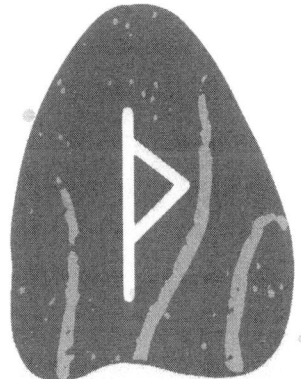

Keywords:

Reaction, Defense, Conflict, Catharsis, Regeneration.

_____

_____

_____

_____

_____

_____

_____

_____

_____

_____

Rune Workbook

THURISAZ

Thorn

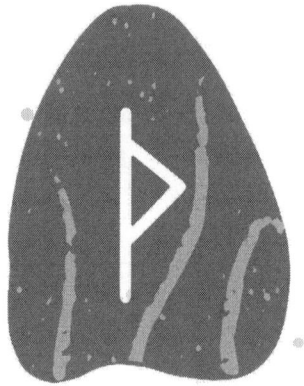

Keywords:

Reaction, Defense, Conflict, Catharsis, Regeneration.

_____

_____

_____

_____

_____

_____

_____

_____

_____

_____

RUNE WORKBOOK

THURISAZ

Thorn

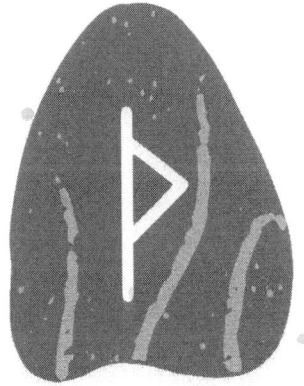

Keywords:

Reaction, Defense, Conflict, Catharsis, Regeneration.

_____

_____

_____

_____

_____

_____

_____

_____

_____

_____

Rune Workbook

ANSUZ

Mouth

Keywords:

Stability, Communication, Understanding, Inspiration.

_____

_____

_____

_____

_____

_____

_____

_____

_____

_____

RUNE WORKBOOK

ANSUZ

Mouth

Keywords:

Stability, Communication, Understanding, Inspiration.

_____

_____

_____

_____

_____

_____

_____

_____

_____

_____

Rune Workbook

ANSUZ

Mouth

Keywords:

Stability, Communication, Understanding, Inspiration.

_____

_____

_____

_____

_____

_____

_____

_____

_____

Rune Workbook

ANSUZ

Mouth

Keywords:

Stability, Communication, Understanding, Inspiration.

_____

_____

_____

_____

_____

_____

_____

_____

_____

_____

Rune Workbook

RAIDHO

Wheel

Keywords:

Travel, Rhythm, Spontaneity, Evolution, Decisions, Achieving Goals.

_____
_____
_____
_____
_____
_____
_____
_____
_____
_____

Rune Workbook

RAIDHO

Wheel

Keywords:

Travel, Rhythm, Spontaneity, Evolution, Decisions, Achieving Goals.

_____

_____

_____

_____

_____

_____

_____

_____

_____

RUNE WORKBOOK

RAIDHO

Wheel

Keywords:

Travel, Rhythm, Spontaneity, Evolution, Decisions, Achieving Goals.

_____

_____

_____

_____

_____

_____

_____

_____

_____

Rune Workbook

RAIDHO

Wheel

Keywords:

Travel, Rhythm, Spontaneity, Evolution, Decisions, Achieving Goals.

Rune Workbook

KENNAZ

Torch

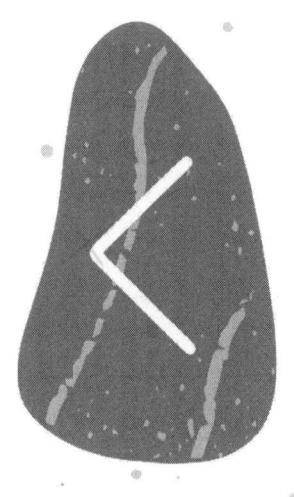

Keywords:

Knowledge, Creativity, Inspiration, Improvement, Vitality, Clarity.

Rune Workbook

KENNAZ

Torch

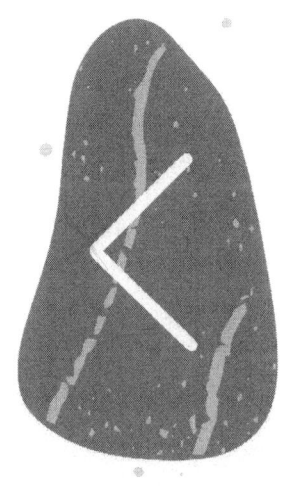

Keywords:

Knowledge, Creativity, Inspiration, Improvement, Vitality, Clarity.

Rune Workbook

KENNAZ

Torch

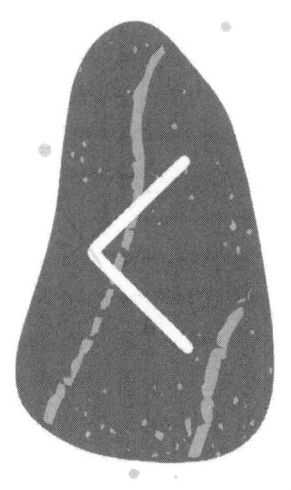

Keywords:

Knowledge, Creativity, Inspiration, Improvement, Vitality, Clarity.

_____

_____

_____

_____

_____

_____

_____

_____

_____

_____

Rune Workbook

KENNAZ

Torch

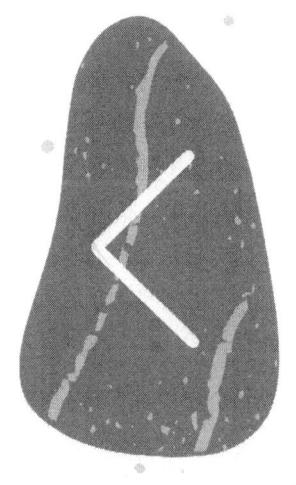

Keywords:

Knowledge, Creativity, Inspiration, Improvement, Vitality, Clarity.

_____

_____

_____

_____

_____

_____

_____

_____

_____

_____

RUNe WORKbooK

GEBO

Gift

Keywords:

Balance, Exchange, Partnership, Generosity, Relationships.

_____

_____

_____

_____

_____

_____

_____

_____

_____

Rune Workbook

GEBO

Gift

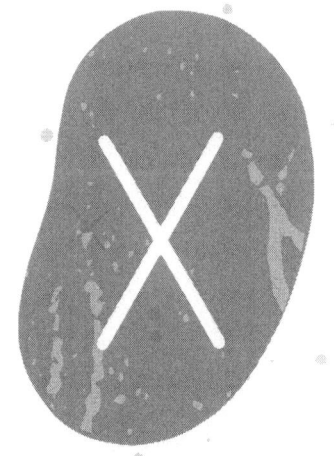

Keywords:

Balance, Exchange, Partnership, Generosity, Relationships.

Rune Workbook

GEBO

Gift

Keywords:

Balance, Exchange, Partnership, Generosity, Relationships.

_____

_____

_____

_____

_____

_____

_____

_____

_____

_____

Rune Workbook

GEBO

Gift

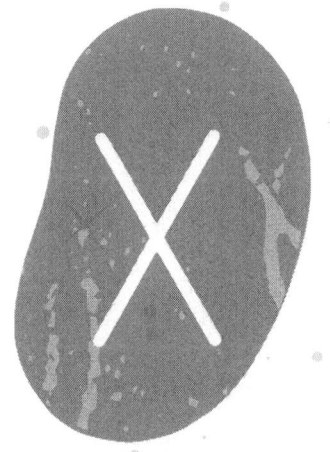

Keywords:

Balance, Exchange, Partnership, Generosity, Relationships.

_____

_____

_____

_____

_____

_____

_____

_____

_____

Rune Workbook

WUNJO

Joy

Keywords:

Good News, Pleasure, Comfort, Harmony, Prosperity, Reward, Success.

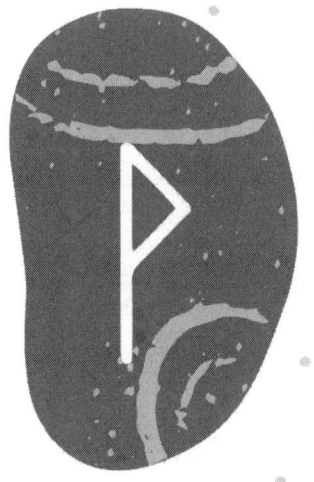

_____

_____

_____

_____

_____

_____

_____

_____

_____

RUNe WORKbooK

WUNJO

Joy

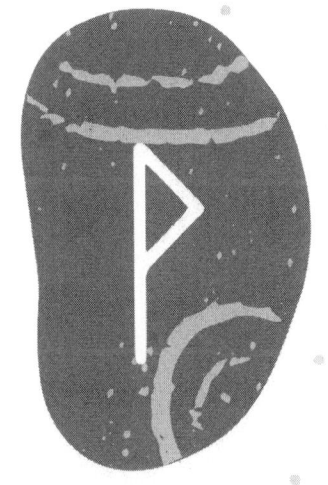

Keywords:

Good News, Pleasure, Comfort, Harmony, Prosperity, Reward, Success.

_____

_____

_____

_____

_____

_____

_____

_____

_____

Rune Workbook

WUNJO

Joy

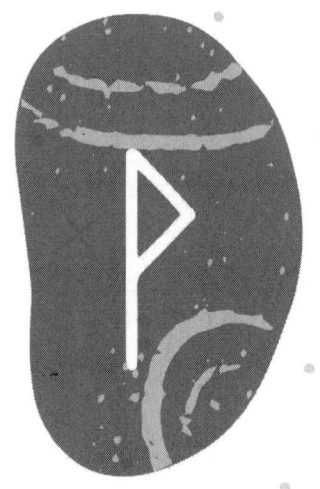

Keywords:

Good News, Pleasure, Comfort, Harmony, Prosperity, Reward, Success.

_____

_____

_____

_____

_____

_____

_____

_____

_____

Rune Workbook

WUNJO

Joy

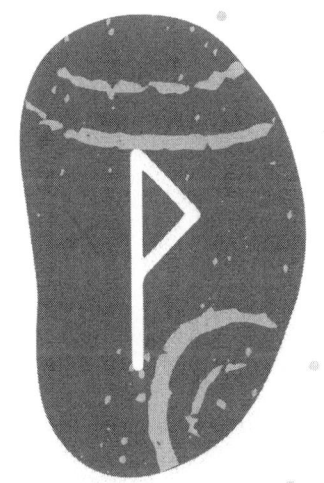

Keywords:

Good News, Pleasure, Comfort, Harmony, Prosperity, Reward, Success.

Rune Workbook

HAGALAZ

Hail

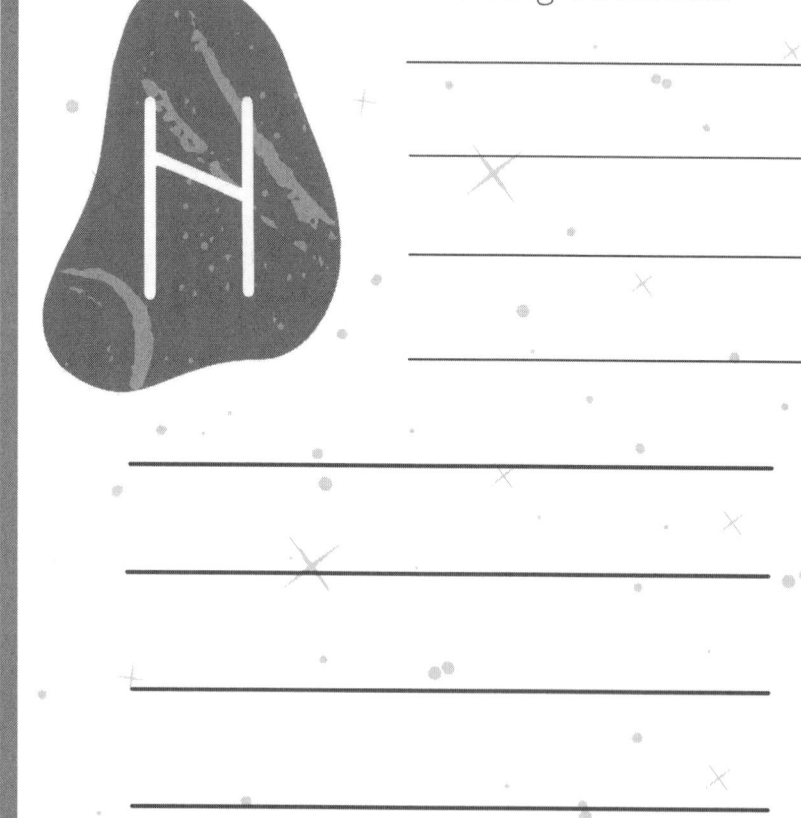

Keywords:

Nature, Wrath, Being Tested, Overcoming Obstacles.

_____

_____

_____

_____

_____

_____

_____

_____

_____

_____

Rune Workbook

HAGALAZ

Hail

Keywords:

Nature, Wrath, Being Tested, Overcoming Obstacles.

_____

_____

_____

_____

_____

_____

_____

_____

_____

_____

Rune Workbook

HAGALAZ

Hail

Keywords:

Nature, Wrath, Being Tested, Overcoming Obstacles.

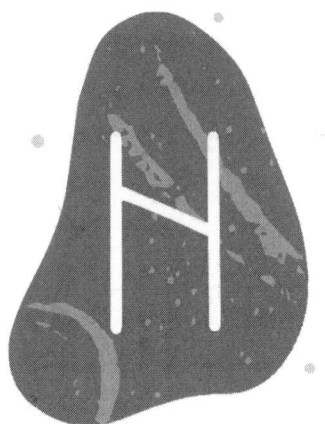

_____

_____

_____

_____

_____

_____

_____

_____

_____

_____

RUNE WORKBOOK

HAGALAZ

Hail

Keywords:

Nature, Wrath, Being Tested, Overcoming Obstacles.

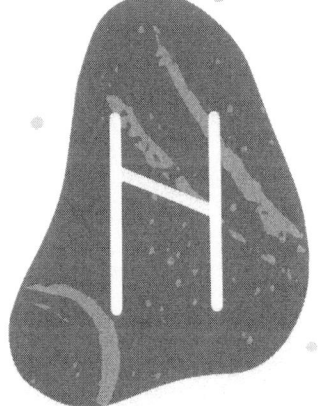

_____

_____

_____

_____

_____

_____

_____

_____

_____

Rune Workbook

NAUTHIZ

Need

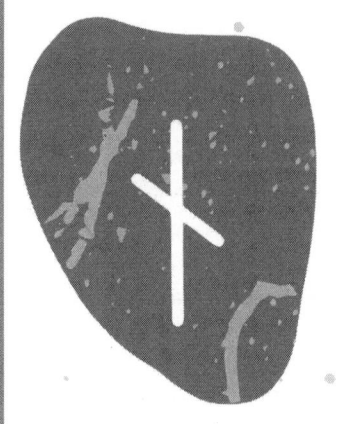

Keywords:

Restriction, Conflict, Willpower, Endurance, Self-Reliance.

_____

_____

_____

_____

_____

_____

_____

_____

_____

_____

Rune Workbook

NAUTHIZ

Need

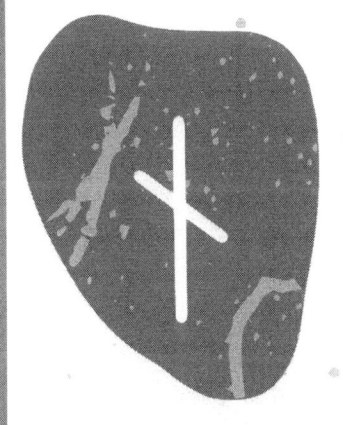

Keywords:

Restriction, Conflict, Willpower, Endurance, Self-Reliance.

_____

_____

_____

_____

_____

_____

_____

_____

_____

_____

Rune Workbook

NAUTHIZ

Need

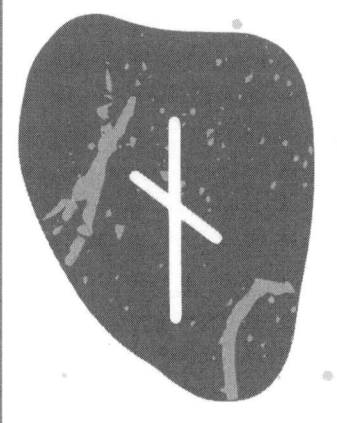

Keywords:

Restriction, Conflict, Willpower, Endurance, Self-Reliance.

_____

_____

_____

_____

_____

_____

_____

_____

_____

_____

Rune Workbook

NAUTHIZ

Need

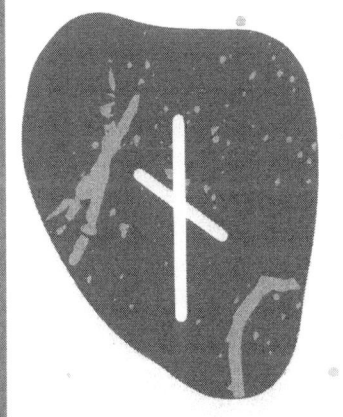

Keywords:

Restriction, Conflict, Willpower, Endurance, Self-Reliance.

_____

_____

_____

_____

_____

_____

_____

_____

_____

_____

RuNe WorKbooK

ISA

Ice

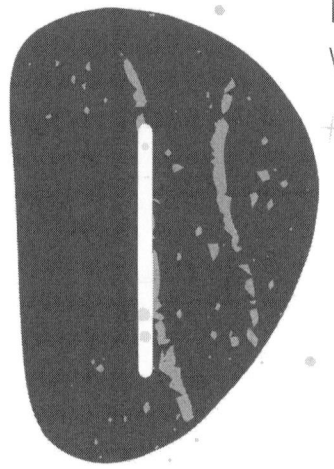

Keywords:

Clarity, Pause, Challenges, Introspection, Watching & Waiting.

Rune Workbook

ISA

Ice

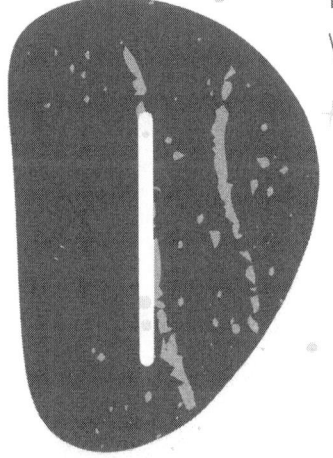

Keywords:

Clarity, Pause, Challenges, Introspection, Watching & Waiting.

_____

_____

_____

_____

_____

_____

_____

_____

_____

_____

Rune Workbook

ISA

Ice

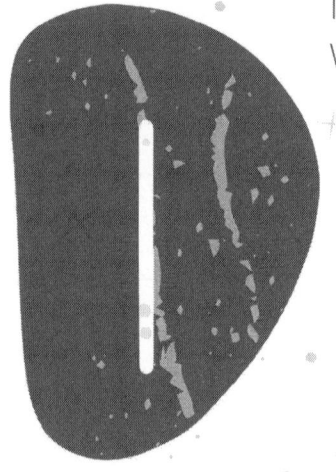

Keywords:

Clarity, Pause, Challenges, Introspection, Watching & Waiting.

_____

_____

_____

_____

_____

_____

_____

_____

_____

Rune Workbook

ISA

Ice

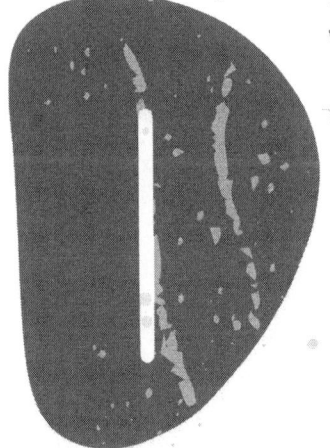

Keywords:

Clarity, Pause, Challenges, Introspection, Watching & Waiting.

_____

_____

_____

_____

_____

_____

_____

_____

_____

_____

RUNE WORKBOOK

JERA

Year

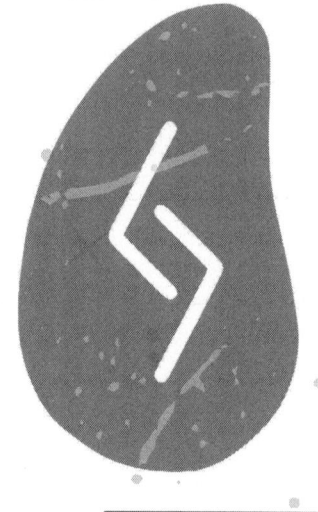

Keywords:

Cycles, Go With The Flow, Completion, Changes, Harvest, Reaping Rewards.

_____

_____

_____

_____

_____

_____

_____

_____

_____

Rune Workbook

JERA

Year

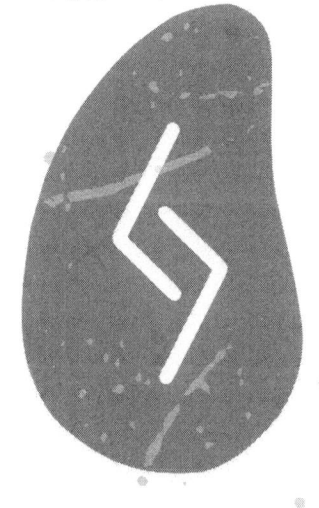

Keywords:

Cycles, Go With The Flow, Completion, Changes, Harvest, Reaping Rewards.

_____

_____

_____

_____

_____

_____

_____

_____

_____

RUNE WORKBOOK

JERA

Year

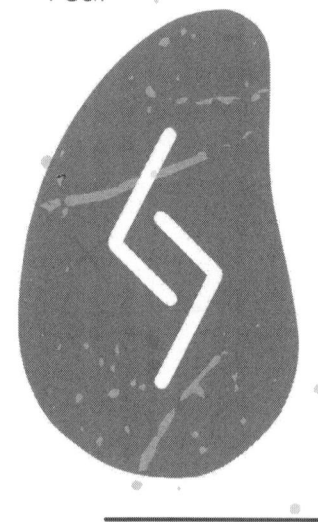

Keywords:

Cycles, Go With The Flow, Completion, Changes, Harvest, Reaping Rewards.

_____

_____

_____

_____

_____

_____

_____

_____

_____

Rune Workbook

JERA

Year

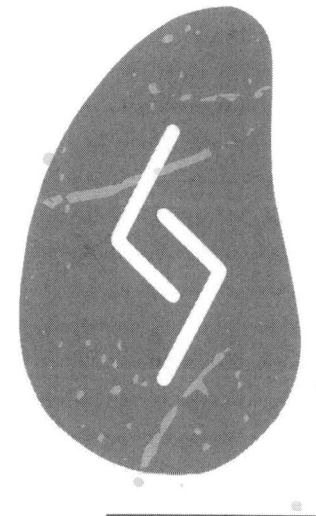

Keywords:

Cycles, Go With The Flow, Completion, Changes, Harvest, Reaping Rewards.

_____

_____

_____

_____

_____

_____

_____

_____

_____

Rune Workbook

EIHWAZ

Yew tree

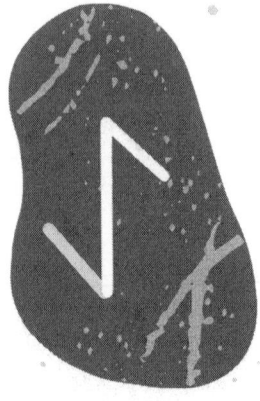

Keywords:

Endings, Balance, Enlightenment, Death, The World Tree.

Rune Workbook

EIHWAZ

Yew tree

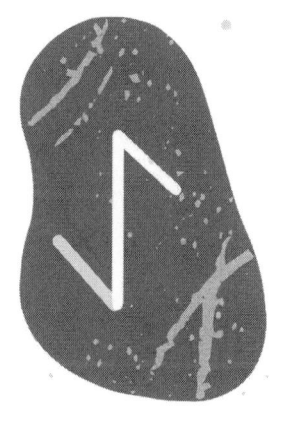

Keywords:

Endings, Balance, Enlightenment, Death, The World Tree.

_____

_____

_____

_____

_____

_____

_____

_____

_____

_____

Rune Workbook

EIHWAZ

Yew tree

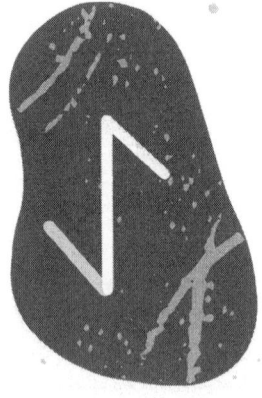

Keywords:

Endings, Balance, Enlightenment, Death, The World Tree.

_____

_____

_____

_____

_____

_____

_____

_____

_____

Rune Workbook

EIHWAZ

Yew tree

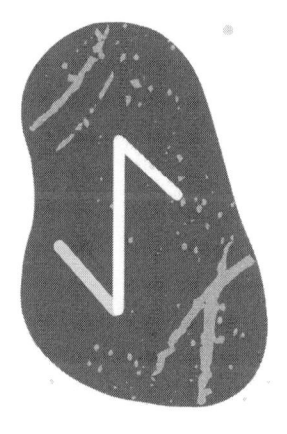

Keywords:

Endings, Balance, Enlightenment, Death, The World Tree.

_____

_____

_____

_____

_____

_____

_____

_____

_____

_____

Rune Workbook

PERTHRO

Dice Cup

Keywords:

Uncertainty, Fate, Chance, Mystery, Destiny, Secrets.

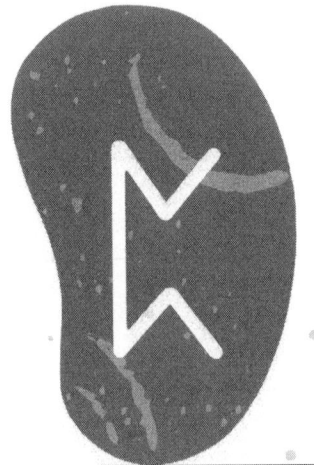

_____

_____

_____

_____

_____

_____

_____

_____

_____

Rune Workbook

PERTHRO

Dice Cup

Keywords:

Uncertainty, Fate, Chance, Mystery, Destiny, Secrets.

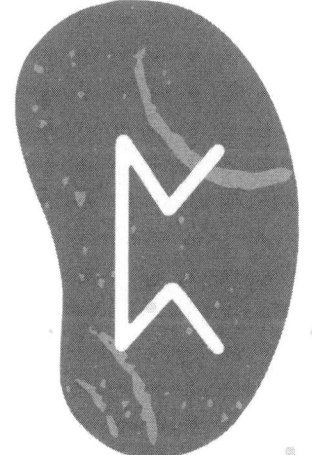

_____

_____

_____

_____

_____

_____

_____

_____

_____

_____

Rune Workbook

PERTHRO

Dice Cup

Keywords:

Uncertainty, Fate, Chance, Mystery, Destiny, Secrets.

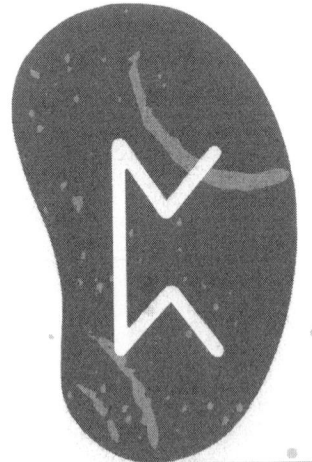

_____

_____

_____

_____

_____

_____

_____

_____

_____

Rune Workbook

PERTHRO

Dice Cup

Keywords:

Uncertainty, Fate, Chance, Mystery, Destiny, Secrets.

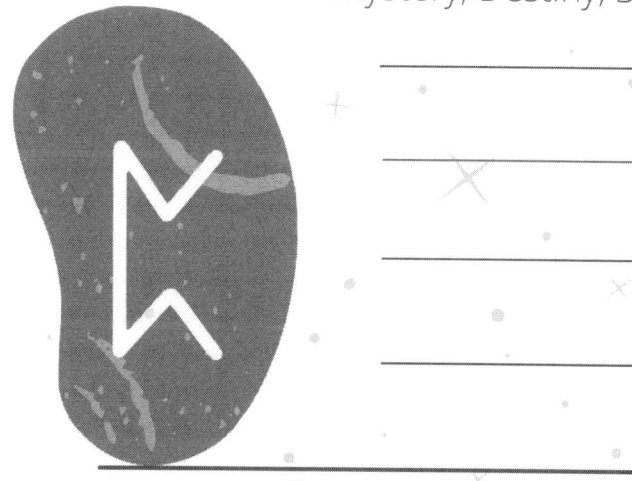

_____

_____

_____

_____

_____

_____

_____

_____

_____

_____

Rune Workbook

ALGIZ

Elk

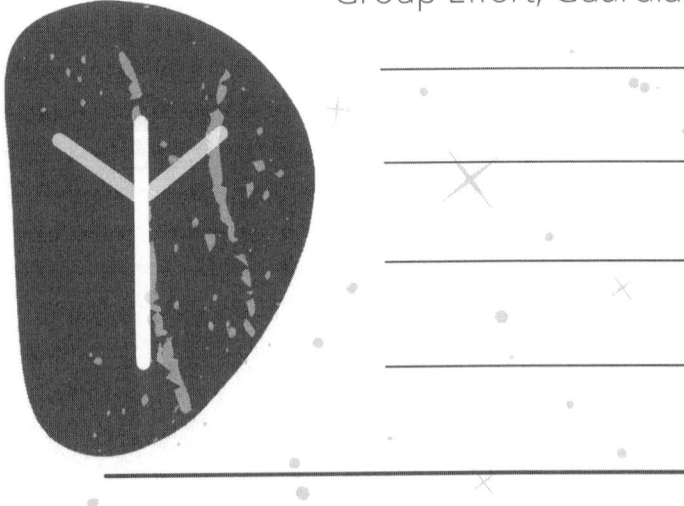

Keywords:

Protection, Defense, Instinct, Group Effort, Guardianship.

_____

_____

_____

_____

_____

_____

_____

_____

_____

Rune Workbook

ALGIZ

Elk

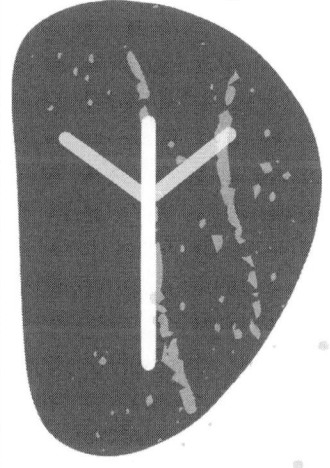

Keywords:

Protection, Defense, Instinct, Group Effort, Guardianship.

_____

_____

_____

_____

_____

_____

_____

_____

_____

_____

Rune Workbook

ALGIZ

Elk

Keywords:

Protection, Defense, Instinct, Group Effort, Guardianship.

_____

_____

_____

_____

_____

_____

_____

_____

_____

Rune Workbook

ALGIZ

Elk

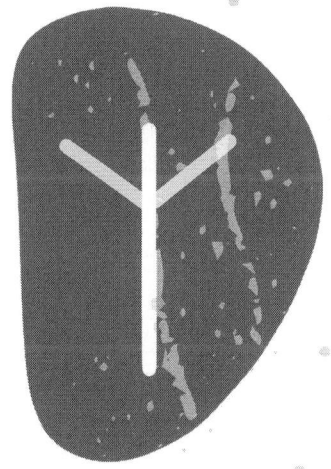

Keywords:

Protection, Defense, Instinct, Group Effort, Guardianship.

_____

_____

_____

_____

_____

_____

_____

_____

_____

Rune Workbook

SOWILO

Sun

Keywords:

Health, Clarity, Resources, Victory, Wholeness, Cleansing.

_____

_____

_____

_____

_____

_____

_____

_____

_____

Rune Workbook

SOWILO

Sun

Keywords:

Health, Clarity, Resources, Victory, Wholeness, Cleansing.

_____

_____

_____

_____

_____

_____

_____

_____

_____

_____

Rune Workbook

SOWILO

Sun

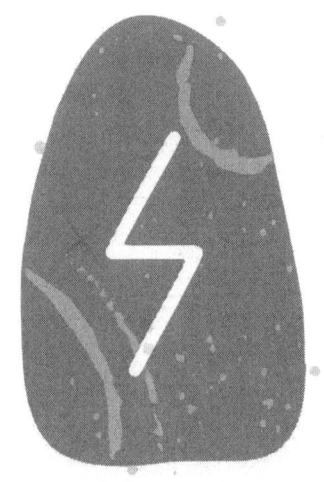

Keywords:

Health, Clarity, Resources, Victory, Wholeness, Cleansing.

RUNE WORKBOOK

SOWILO

Sun

Keywords:

Health, Clarity, Resources, Victory, Wholeness, Cleansing.

Rune Workbook

TIWAZ

God Tyr

Keywords:

Masculinity, Justice, Leadership, Logic, Battle.

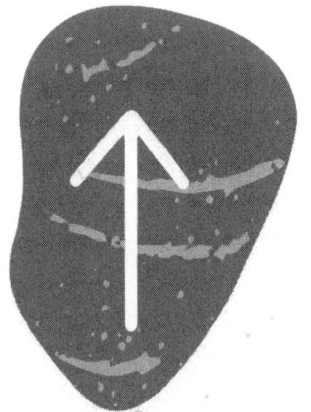

_____

_____

_____

_____

_____

_____

_____

_____

_____

_____

Rune Workbook

TIWAZ

God Tyr

Keywords:

Masculinity, Justice, Leadership, Logic, Battle.

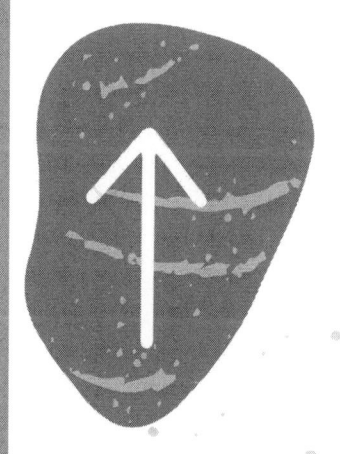

_____

_____

_____

_____

_____

_____

_____

_____

_____

_____

_____

Rune Workbook

TIWAZ

God Tyr

Keywords:

Masculinity, Justice, Leadership, Logic, Battle.

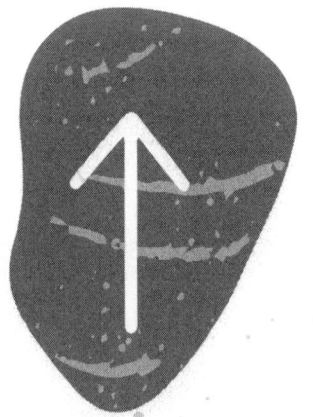

_____

_____

_____

_____

_____

_____

_____

_____

_____

Rune Workbook

TIWAZ

God Tyr

Keywords:

Masculinity, Justice, Leadership, Logic, Battle.

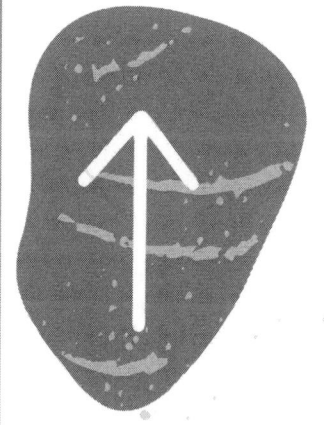

_____

_____

_____

_____

_____

_____

_____

_____

_____

_____

_____

Rune Workbook

BERKANA

Birch Tree

Keywords:

Femininity, Fertility, Healing, Regeneration, Birth.

Rune Workbook

BERKANA

Birch Tree

Keywords:

Femininity, Fertility, Healing, Regeneration, Birth.

_____

_____

_____

_____

_____

_____

_____

_____

_____

_____

_____

Rune Workbook

BERKANA

Birch Tree

Keywords:

Femininity, Fertility, Healing, Regeneration, Birth.

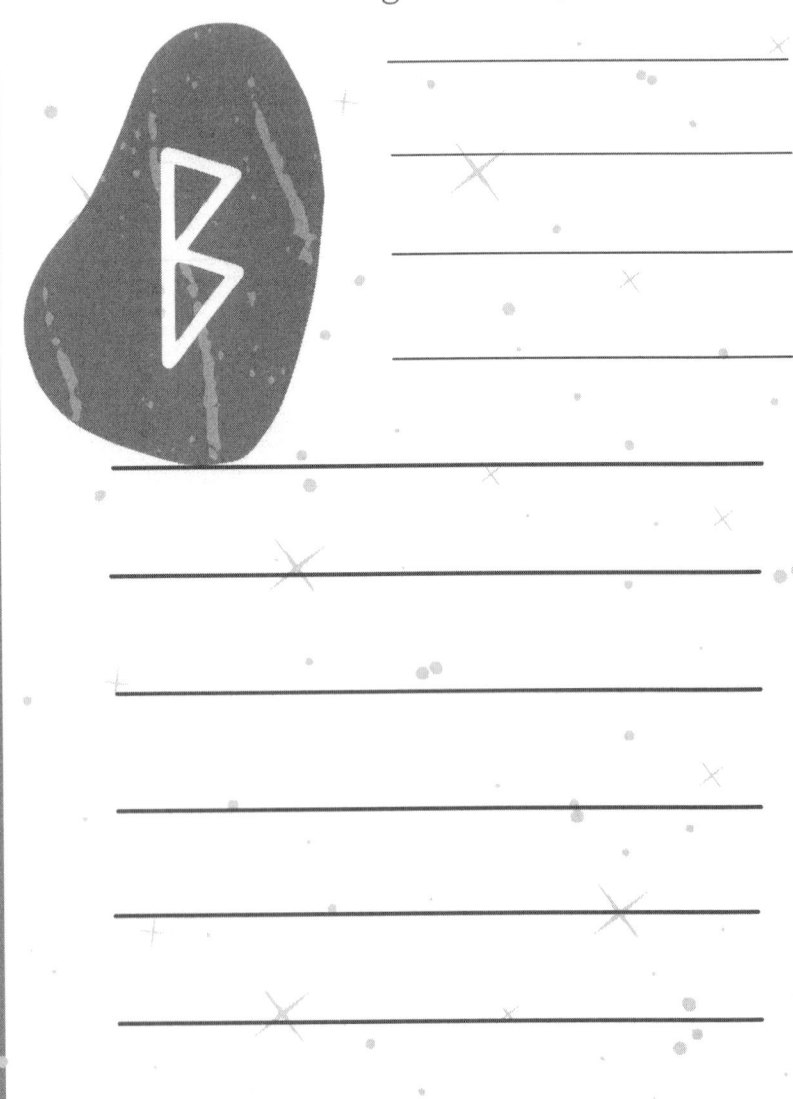

_____

_____

_____

_____

_____

_____

_____

_____

_____

Rune Workbook

BERKANA

Birch Tree

Keywords:

Femininity, Fertility, Healing, Regeneration, Birth.

_____

_____

_____

_____

_____

_____

_____

_____

_____

_____

Rune Workbook

EHWAZ

Horse

Keywords:

Power, Transportation, Movement, Progress, Trust, Change.

Rune Workbook

EHWAZ

Horse

Keywords:

Power, Transportation, Movement, Progress, Trust, Change.

Rune Workbook

EHWAZ

Horse

Keywords:

Power, Transportation, Movement, Progress, Trust, Change.

_____

_____

_____

_____

_____

_____

_____

_____

Rune Workbook

EHWAZ

Horse

Keywords:

Power, Transportation, Movement, Progress, Trust, Change.

_____

_____

_____

_____

_____

_____

_____

_____

_____

Rune Workbook

MANNAZ

Humanity

Keywords:

Sharing, Friendship, Society, Cooperation, Help.

_____

_____

_____

_____

_____

_____

_____

_____

_____

RUNE WORKBOOK

MANNAZ

Humanity

Keywords:

Sharing, Friendship, Society, Cooperation, Help.

_____

_____

_____

_____

_____

_____

_____

_____

_____

_____

Rune Workbook

MANNAZ

Humanity

Keywords:

Sharing, Friendship, Society, Cooperation, Help.

_____

_____

_____

_____

_____

_____

_____

_____

_____

Rune Workbook

MANNAZ

Humanity

Keywords:

Sharing, Friendship, Society, Cooperation, Help.

_____

_____

_____

_____

_____

_____

_____

_____

_____

Rune Workbook

LAGUZ

Water

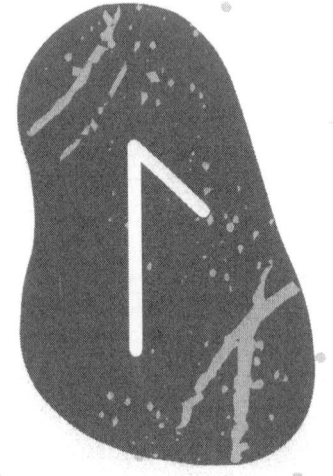

Keywords:

Intuition, Emotions, Go With The Flow, Renewal, Dreams, Hopes & Fears.

_____

_____

_____

_____

_____

_____

_____

_____

Rune Workbook

LAGUZ

Water

Keywords:

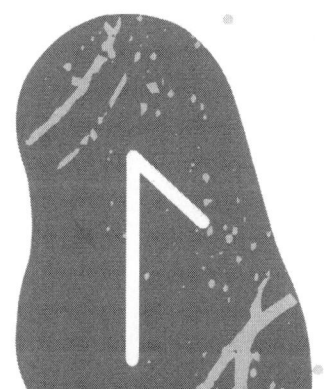

Intuition, Emotions, Go With The Flow, Renewal, Dreams, Hopes & Fears.

_____

_____

_____

_____

_____

_____

_____

_____

_____

Rune Workbook

LAGUZ

Water

Keywords:

Intuition, Emotions, Go With The Flow, Renewal, Dreams, Hopes & Fears.

_____

_____

_____

_____

_____

_____

_____

_____

_____

Rune Workbook

LAGUZ

Water

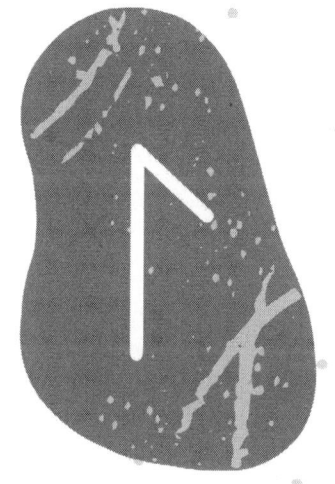

Keywords:

Intuition, Emotions, Go With The Flow, Renewal, Dreams, Hopes & Fears.

_____

_____

_____

_____

_____

_____

_____

_____

_____

Rune Workbook

INGUZ

Seed

Keywords:

Fertility, Goals, Growth, Change, Common Sense, The Hearth (Home).

_____
_____
_____
_____
_____
_____
_____
_____

Rune Workbook

INGUZ

Seed

Keywords:

Fertility, Goals, Growth, Change, Common Sense, The Hearth (Home).

Rune Workbook

INGUZ

Seed

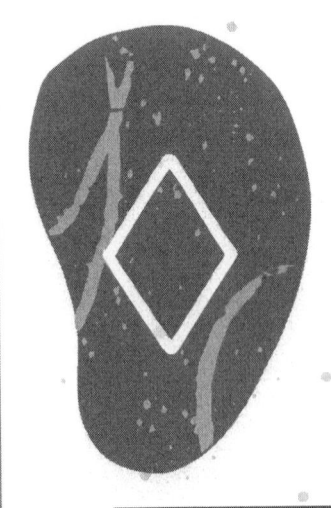

Keywords:

Fertility, Goals, Growth, Change, Common Sense, The Hearth (Home).

_____

_____

_____

_____

_____

_____

_____

_____

_____

Rune Workbook

INGUZ

Seed

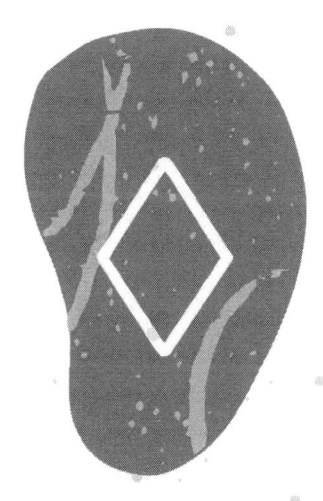

Keywords:

Fertility, Goals, Growth, Change, Common Sense, The Hearth (Home).

Rune Workbook

DAGAZ

Day

Keywords:

Breakthrough, Awakening, Certainty, Illumination, Completion, Hope.

Rune Workbook

DAGAZ

Day

Keywords:

Breakthrough, Awakening, Certainty, Illumination, Completion, Hope.

Rune Workbook

DAGAZ

Day

Keywords:

Breakthrough, Awakening, Certainty, Illumination, Completion, Hope.

Rune Workbook

DAGAZ

Day

Keywords:

Breakthrough, Awakening, Certainty, Illumination, Completion, Hope.

Rune Workbook

OTHALA

Ancestral Property

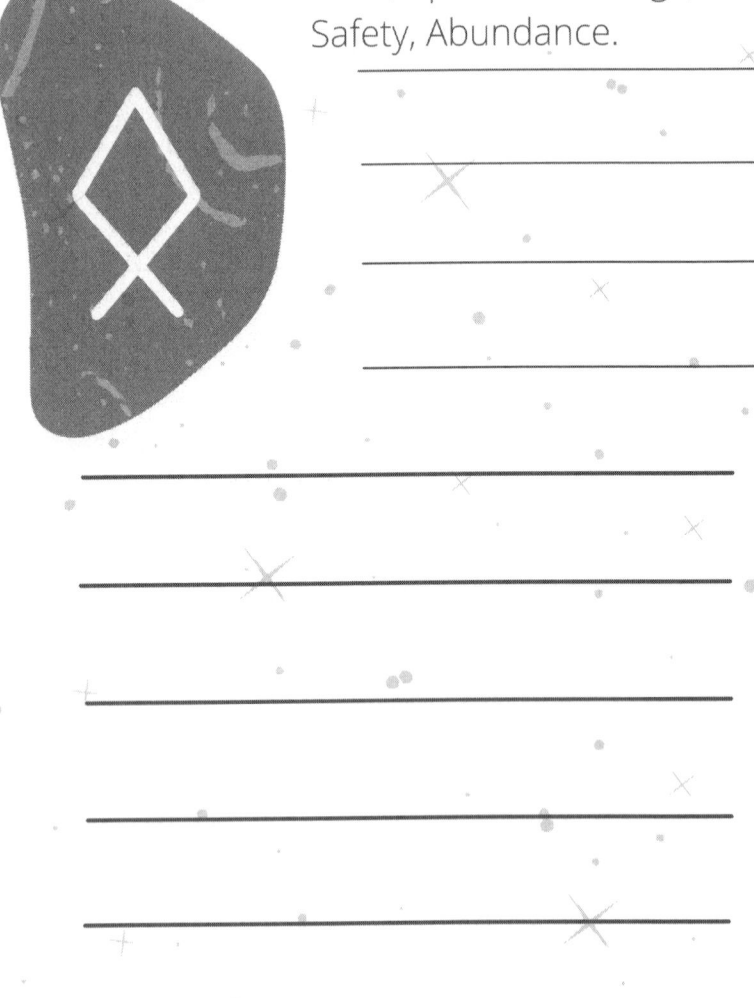

Keywords:

Inheritance, Property, Home, Land, Spiritual Heritage, Safety, Abundance.

_____

_____

_____

_____

_____

_____

_____

_____

_____

RUNE WORKBOOK

OTHALA

Ancestral Property

Keywords: Inheritance, Property, Home, Land, Spiritual Heritage, Safety, Abundance.

Rune Workbook

OTHALA

Ancestral Property

Keywords: Inheritance, Property, Home, Land, Spiritual Heritage, Safety, Abundance.

_____

_____

_____

_____

_____

_____

_____

_____

_____

_____

Rune Workbook

OTHALA

Ancestral Property

Keywords: Inheritance, Property, Home, Land, Spiritual Heritage, Safety, Abundance.

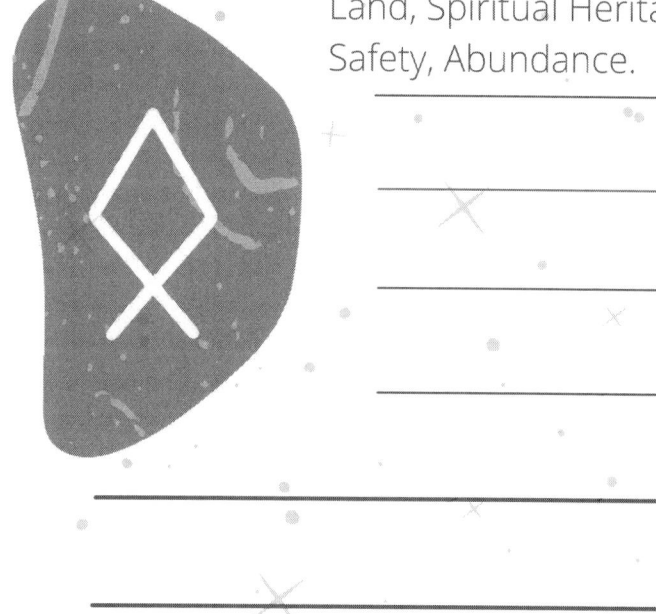

_____

_____

_____

_____

_____

_____

_____

_____

_____

_____

Printed in Great Britain
by Amazon